SCIENCE ON THE LOOSE

Amazing Activities and Science Facts You'll Never Believe

Helaine Becker

Illustrated by Claudia Dávila

MAPLE
TREE
PRESS

Maple Tree Press Inc.
51 Front Street East, Suite 200, Toronto, Ontario M5E 1B3
www.mapletreepress.com

Distributed in Canada by Raincoast Books
9050 Shaughnessy Street, Vancouver, British Columbia V6P 6E5

Distributed in the United States by Publishers Group West
1700 Fourth Street, Berkeley, California 94710

Dedication
For Andrew and Michael

Cataloguing in Publication Data
Becker, Helaine, 1961–
    Science on the loose : amazing activities and science facts you'll never believe / Helaine Becker ; Claudia Dávila, illustrator and designer.

Includes index.
ISBN 978-1-897349-18-2 (bound).—ISBN 978-1-897349-19-9 (pbk.)

1. Science—Juvenile literature. 2. Science—Experiments—Juvenile literature. I. Dávila, Claudia II. Title.

Q164.B43 2008   j500   C2007-906069-2

Library of Congress Control Number: 2007939081

Design: Claudia Dávila
Illustrations: Claudia Dávila

ONTARIO ARTS COUNCIL
CONSEIL DES ARTS DE L'ONTARIO

We acknowledge the financial support of the Canada Council for the Arts, the Ontario Arts Council, the Government of Canada through the Book Publishing Industry Development Program (BPIDP), and the Government of Ontario through the Ontario Media Development Corporation's Book Initiative for our publishing activities.

The activities in this book have been tested and are safe when conducted as instructed. The author and publisher accept no responsibility for any damage caused or sustained by the use or misuse of ideas or material featured in *Science on the Loose*.

Printed in China

A   B   C   D   E   F

CONTENTS

LET YOUR INNER SCIENTIST LOOSE

Have you ever asked yourself a question that others might find a little weird? Like, "How many times a day do people blink?" or "What makes a chicken cross the road?"

Do you know who asks weird questions—all the time? A scientist! But why should scientists have all the fun? You don't need to wait until you're a grown-up to find out the answer to pressing questions like "Why can't I walk through a wall?" or "Could I make a chimpanzee yawn?" And you don't need fancy lab equipment to do serious science experiments that answer questions like "Do girls pass more wind than boys?"

If you follow a few steps (see right), you can do serious science, even if your subject matter may seem a little goofy. So get out your lab coat, put on your goggles, and mess up your hair. It's time for a visit to the **laff**oratory—sorry!—the **lab**oratory.

In the pages that follow, you'll find loads of really kooky experiments you can do on your own. You can also check out some of the goofiest experiments ever performed—all in the name of science.

The Scientific Method

In just four simple steps, you'll be on your way to solving the scientific mysteries of the universe.

1 Start with a clear question. Whether you want to find the cure for the common cold, or discover the secret to big burps, all science experiments begin with a clear question. For example: why does Lucy make such super-sized burps after lunch?

2 Create a good hypothesis. The next step is coming up with a hypothesis — one possible answer to your question. A good hypothesis might be: the secret to Lucy's big burps is that she swallows a lot of air while eating.

3 Test the hypothesis. This is the tough part: figuring out an experiment that will test your theory. Could you count each time Lucy swallows, and see if there is a relationship between the number of swallows and the size of the burp?

4 Record your findings and repeat the experiment. Your experiment might prove that swallowing air is a big burp inducer. Or it might not. Either way, prepare to test, test, and test again. You may have to change your hypothesis a few times before you find one that you can prove is correct. Keep good records so someone else can repeat your experiment.

LOST iN YOUR SPACE...

Is there anything more fascinating than you, marvelous you? Of course not. So why not begin your scientific explorations by learning more about your magnificent self?

Do you know where your arms or legs are at this very minute? And how do you know? Your brain relies on a sense called **proprioception** to determine the position of your body parts in space. Receptors in your muscles, joints, eyes, and ears work together to tell your brain: "stretched out on sofa, remote in left hand," or "fingers in cookie dough." Try some of these sense-sational activities to see your proprioception sensors in action.

RING AROUND ROSIE

Before you squeeze into a space, you need to decide if you can fit in it, right? Your sense of proprioception tells you how much room your body takes up in space. How accurate is your body-size sense?

1 Arrange the jump rope in a large circle on the floor.

2 Watch as your friends slowly tug on either end of the rope to pull the circle smaller and smaller. At the point when you think the rope circle on the floor matches the size of your waist, shout "Stop!" Your friends will stop tightening the rope circle.

3 Carefully step into the circle. Without changing its size, lift the rope so it is around your waist. Did you guess correctly? Most people don't! We tend to think we are a lot larger than we are.

YOU'LL NEED

a jump (skipping) rope
~
2 friends

What's Going On?

Researchers don't know exactly why most people have a distorted body-size image. Some think that we all have an inner idea of what a body looks like. As we grow, we constantly adjust that mental image of "human body" to fit our own. The brain can have trouble matching up the ideal to the real figure—especially if your body is changing a lot, like when you are a growing kid.

Big Word Hotline:
"Proprioception" comes from two Latin words: *proprius*, which means "one's own," and *perceptio*, which means "the act of being able to perceive and understand."

PINK FLAMINGOS NEED NOT APPLY

How important is vision to proprioception? Do this unbalanced experiment for a real eye-opener.

YOU'LL NEED

a friend
~
clock with a second hand

1 Stand on one leg, flamingo-style.

2 Stay in this position for 30 seconds without putting your other foot back on the ground.

3 Repeat the experiment—this time with your eyes closed!

4 Can you keep your balance? Make sure to give your friend a chance to try!

THE FLOATING ARM

Try this uplifting experiment to see how your brain and muscles react when your body-position sensors are triggered.

YOU'LL NEED

a wall

1 Lean against the wall so the side of one arm is pressed tightly against it.

2 Push your arm hard against the wall, as if you were trying to raise your arm away from your body, for about 30 to 60 seconds.

3 Close your eyes.

4 Step away from the wall.

5 Your arm will "magically" seem to float up in the air!

What's Going On?

When you press your arm into the wall, you're tightening (contracting) muscles that would raise your arm if it weren't restrained. Once you step away from the wall, the muscles relax, then automatically contract again. Without the downward pressure on your arm, the contracting muscles float the arm up.

No Peeking

Your eyes send visual cues to your brain that can override the automatic effect, so this experiment works best when you can't see your arm.

FOOL YOUR BRAIN — FOR SCIENCE

Now that you've seen your proprioception sensors in action, what do you think would happen if your body's space sensors got a confusing message? What if your brain gets information that is garbled, incomplete, or total nonsense? Find out by playing tricks on your sense of proprioception.

MIXED UP MIRROR MAGIC

Where your brain is concerned, seeing really is believing. So what happens when what you're seeing and hearing don't add up for your brain? Try this mixed-up mind game to find out.

YOU'LL NEED

mirror, about 30 cm x 30 cm (12 in. x 12 in.)

1. Sitting at a table, prop the mirror up on the table in front of you, with the mirrored side facing right (you might need some small blocks or a couple of books on either side to hold it up).

2. Lay your arms out along the table in front of you, with the mirror standing up in between them.

3. Now tilt your head so you can look into the mirror. You see two arms (though the one in the mirror is really the reflection of your right arm).

4. Snap the fingers on your left and right hands at the same time. Then stop snapping your right hand. Do you get a very weird sensation as you watch two still (non-snapping) hands in the mirror but continue to hear a snapping sound?

The Famous Rubber Hand Experiment

Researchers at Carnegie Mellon Institute fooled subjects into thinking a rubber arm was their own! In their experiment, the scientists hid the subject's arm beneath a cover and placed a fake arm nearby. They then used tiny brushes to stroke the subject's real, hidden arm. At the same time, they stroked the rubber arm in plain view. As the subjects watched the rubber arm, they began to believe it was their own arm. Afterwards, when asked to touch their real arm, they missed! They aimed for where the rubber arm had been.

Great, now I'm all itchy.

ACME RUBBER LIMBS INC.

The Spin Cycle

In an open space, close your eyes and spin for 10 to 15 seconds. Then try to walk in a straight line. Do you feel dizzy? Here's why: Your inner ear is like a cup, lined with tiny, hairlike sense receptors. Fluid in the "cup" moves as you move. The motion of the fluid on the receptors tells your brain about your body's position. When you spin, so does the fluid. Even after you stop, the fluid swirls for a few more seconds. So receptors tell your brain: "I'm still spinning!" even when you've stopped.

Try It!

You can simulate motion's effect on your inner ear by filling a glass part way with water. Gently swirl the water in the glass until you get a whirlpool going. Then hold the glass still. How long after you've stopped moving the glass does the water stop moving?

What's Going On?

It's all about mixed messages. Your eyes, watching two hands in the mirror, are sending your brain one message: "My hands aren't moving." But your ears and the muscles of your left hand are sending another message: "I'm snapping my fingers." The weird sensation you feel is your confused brain trying to make sense of these mixed-up mirror messages.

SNAP! SNAP! SNAP!

MORE FOOLING

Are you ready to boggle your brain again?
These experiments show you even more ways
that your brilliant brain can be fooled.

THE UNRELIABLE EYE WITNESS EXPERIMENT

Imagine you are the witness to a theft. You need to tell the police exactly what you saw written on the robber's shirt. Can you really trust your own eyes?

Look at the image to the right. The figure in the middle is what was marked on the robber's shirt. What is it? Remember, this is the information you will be reporting to the police officer.

Now look at the image below. Are you still sure that what you saw was the letter B?

12 13 14

Did you change your mind? Is the shape the letter B, or the number 13?

What's Going On?

What your brain perceives is affected by what else is going on at the time. For example, if you saw a person shouting at an exciting baseball game, you might think he is having fun. But if you saw the same person shouting into his phone on the street, you might think he is angry. The action (shouting) stays the same, but the situation, or context, changes. And this changes how you understand what you see. For more on context, see page 41.

Pass It to the Gorilla!

You're watching a basketball game when a gorilla runs across the court. Would you notice it? Maybe not. Researchers at Harvard University conducted an experiment to test whether or not people who are focusing hard on something—like watching an exciting basketball game—would perceive something out of the ordinary—like the gorilla. So they staged an experiment in which subjects were told to watch a game and count how many times the basketball was passed between players. During the experiment, a woman in a gorilla suit ran across the court. Nearly half (46%) of the viewers failed to notice the gorilla!

Try It!

Look at the picture to the right. Do you see a gray square above, and a white square below? Now lay two fingers across the picture to hide the boundary between the two colored squares. Are they still different colors?

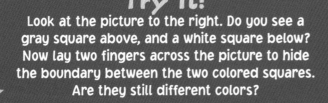

Think About It

If our brains can be "tricked" by context and distractions, how reliable are eyewitnesses to crimes?

HOW TOUCHING...

Sandpaper or velvet? Fire or ice?
Touch receptors are what allow you to tell the difference.

Touch receptors send signals to the brain about any object that touches your body. For example, if a mysterious substance presses up against your left hand, your touch sensors might send these signals: soft + wet + cool + windy.

The brain then analyzes the signals. It matches them to information stored in your memory banks. It then comes up with a conclusion and an appropriate reaction: soft + wet + cool + windy = aha! Dog's nose! Appropriate reaction: pat Scruffy on head.

But what if the signals are not clear? What's a poor brain to do when a weird message comes through? Find out by performing the touching experiments on these pages.

wet + cold + slippery = my guppy

Feeling Touchy?

Touch receptors are located in the lower layer of your skin. There are several different types. Some are sensitive to pain; others react to heat or cold. Still others are sensitive to pressure. Not all parts of your body have equal numbers of every kind of receptor. Your tongue, for example, has lots of pain receptors. That's why it hurts so much if you accidentally chomp down on it. It has far fewer heat and cold receptors, though, than other parts of your body, like your fingertips. That's why it's so easy to burn your tongue when you bite into that hot-from-the-oven pizza.

ARISTOTLE'S CROSSED FINGERS

Test your sense of touch with this trick, described by the Greek philosopher Aristotle more than 2,000 years ago.

YOU'LL NEED

nothing but curiosity

1 Cross the middle finger of your favorite hand over the index finger, like you might do as a symbol for luck.

2 Close your eyes.

3 Touch the bridge of your nose with the "V" between your crossed fingers. (You might need to use your other hand to guide your fingers to the right place.) Slowly slide your fingers down your nose. Does it feel strange? Almost like you are touching two noses?

What's Going On?

Your fingers on your right hand line up so that the right side of your pointer and the left side of your middle finger touch (it's the opposite on your left hand). When objects rub the skin on these parts of your fingers, your brain knows that you are probably touching one object between them. But when you cross your fingers, your brain thinks, since the outsides of each finger are being touched, there must be two separate objects—in this case, two noses!

PICKY PICKY PICKY

Sensory receptors are not evenly placed on your skin. In more sensitive areas, like your hands, they are closer together. Less sensitive areas, like your upper back, have fewer receptors, spaced farther apart. To test this:

YOU'LL NEED

2 toothpicks
~
a friend
~
ruler
~
pen and paper for recording your findings

1 Have a friend use two toothpicks to very gently touch the skin on your upper back about 15 cm (6 in.) apart. Can you feel two distinct touches?

2 Your friend should gradually bring the toothpicks closer together, about 1 cm ($1/2$ in.) each time.

3 At a point, you will no longer feel two toothpicks, but just one! This is the distance between two touch receptors on your back. Measure the distance and write it down on your piece of paper.

4 Close your eyes and repeat the test, this time while your friend touches you in the same way on your hand, upper arm, and foot. Record how far apart the toothpicks are when you feel only a "single" prick.

5 Don't forget to repeat the experiments on your friend, and compare your results!

ON ONE CONDITION

Imagine this: you are sitting at your desk in school. The bell rings. It's recess! Do you feel a wave of excitement, slam your books shut, and jump to your feet without even thinking? If so, you have just experienced the effect of conditioning.

RECESS!

RINGGGG!

If the same series of events happen again and again, your brain can learn that when a certain thing happens (like a bell ringing), another thing will probably follow (recess). If that same sequence repeats often enough, when the first event occurs (the bell), it automatically triggers your body to prepare for the second (recess). Adrenalin gushes out of your adrenal glands so you feel excited and primed for action; muscles in your arms and legs contract, in just the right pattern, to lift you out of your chair. Many responses, even ones you don't think about, such as producing saliva or contracting your pupils (see page 28), can be conditioned. It's called the Pavlovian reflex. Why? Read on.

The Case of the Drooling Dogs

In the 1890s, Ivan Pavlov, a Russian scientist, noticed that the dogs he was studying in his lab started to drool long before they were given any food. Why? It turned out that the people who served the dogs food wore lab coats. So whenever the dogs saw people in lab coats, they reacted as if the actual food appeared. Ta dah! White coats = supper!

Pavlov did a lot of experiments with the salivating dogs that helped him develop the groundbreaking theory of conditioning. He discovered much of what we know about how people and animals learn.

Think About It

A lot of popular advertising works on the principle of conditioning. Advertisers hope that through their ads, you will start to associate a particular product (like a tooth whitener) with a positive idea shown in the ad (like popularity).

CONDITIONING = TRAINING

If you have a pet or know someone who does, you can ask to work with the animal to train, or condition, it. Dogs, cats, hamsters, gerbils—even fish!—can be conditioned if you repeat your training exercises often enough.

1 Choose a regular time of day when you can feed the animal.

2 Choose a new place where you will feed the animal. For an animal that lives in a tank, such as a hamster or fish, choose a new corner of the tank. For a cat or dog, move the food bowl to a different location (one the animal can still find easily).

3 Feed the animal every day, at the same time, in the same new location.

4 Observe the animal before you deliver the food and after. Record your observations in a chart in your notebook.

Date	Time	Location of cat before food was delivered	Length of time until cat arrived at food site	Comments
May 14th	8:20 am	Fluffy was in the living room	4 minutes	She didn't notice the food
May 15th	8:15 am	In the living room	1 minute	She's learning!

Training an animal can take a long time—even months. How long depends on how consistent you are and how intelligent the animal is. But as your experiment continues, you might discover that the time it takes for your pet to arrive at the feeding site gets shorter and shorter. You might even find Fluffy waiting for you when you arrive with her food.

Fluffy want FOOD!

TEST YOUR REFLEXES

Producing drool, like Pavlov's dogs, doesn't require any thought—it's an automatic reflex. People, like dogs, have many other reflexes besides the ability to slobber. Go ahead and test some of yours. These simple experiments will produce some dramatic results.

KARATE KNEE

YOU'LL NEED

a friend

1 Your friend sits on a couch or chair with his or her legs crossed. The leg on top should be able to swing freely.

2 Using the side of your hand (like you were making a "karate chop"), gently tap your friend's leg just below the knee. Watch out! If you hit the right place, your friend's leg will kick!

What's Going On?

This reflex is called the knee jerk. When you tap on the tendon below the knee, it causes the muscle in your thigh to automatically contract. Boing! The tightened muscle pulls up on your knee and your legs kicks out! Doctors test this reflex frequently to make sure that your nerves and muscles are working together properly.

MADE YOU BLINK

YOU'LL NEED

access to both
sides of a closed
window

~

a cotton ball

~

a friend

1 Stand on one side of a window. Have your friend stand on the other side.

2 Toss the cotton ball at the window, aiming at your friend's face on the other side.

3 The cotton ball can't hit your friend — there's a pane of glass between you, right? It doesn't matter! Your friend will probably blink anyway. Now you try.

What's Going On?

Your friend just demonstrated the blink reflex. This reflex prevents your eyes from injuries.

You blink
on average
15 times
a minute!

Brain...Who Needs It?

Reflexes happen without your needing to think about them. So why bother with the brain? Guess what: reflexes don't! Simple reflexes—like the knee jerk or pulling back your hand when you touch something hot—are controlled by the spinal cord. Because they don't go through the brain, the reflex messages travel a shorter distance and are processed very quickly.

Hey, wait
til I get to
the window!

NAVEL GAZING

Everyone's got one.... A belly button, that is. Who knew so much science could fit into such a little hole?

Delphi, the holiest site in ancient Greece, was thought to be the world's "omphalos." That's Greek for navel.

The Lowdown on Lint

Did you know that you are more likely to have belly button lint if you have an innie? In a survey conducted by Dr. Karl Kruszelnicki, an Australian scientist and author, it was discovered that the people with the largest amount of button baggage were hairy older men. Hold on, there's more! The survey also confirmed that most belly button lint is blue. The color most likely comes from fluff that rubs off from your clothes, and blue is the most popular clothing shade.

You Collect It?

Graham Barker has been collecting and storing his own belly button lint for more than 20 years. He now has **three containers of BBF** (belly button fluff), which comes to a whopping 1.1 grams (.04 oz) of gunk per year.

INNIE OR OUTIE

Don't be surprised if your belly button looks different from your friends'. Like fingerprints, no two people have the same belly button shape! The most noticeable difference between belly buttons is whether you have any "innie" (like a dimple) or an "outie" (a little bump that sticks out). About 90% of people have innies. Try your own science experiment to find out if your numbers agree!

YOU'LL NEED

paper and pen
~
lots of willing participants
~
a calculator

Unsolved Science

Scientists don't know why some people have innies and others have outies. There are only theories. Some say it depends on where your **umbilical cord** was clipped off when you were born. Others say outies are caused by small tears in the muscles of your abdomen. Are you the future scientist who will discover the answer?

1 Draw a chart with two columns on your paper.

2 Label one column "innie." Label the other column "outie."

3 Ask people you know—the more the better—if they have an innie or an outie. Record each answer on the correct column on your chart.

4 When you have finished collecting your data, add up the total for each column. Record it in the last row.

5 Add together the two numbers from each column. This figure is the total number of people you interviewed (interviewees).

6 What percentage of people have innies? Divide the number of innies by the total number of interviewees. Multiply by 100, and round off your answer.

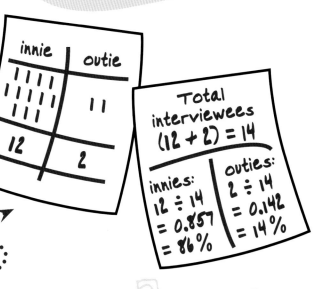

What's Going On?

Are your findings similar to those of other belly button scientists? Keep in mind, the larger the number of people you interview (this is called "the sample size") the more accurate your findings will be.

SCIENTISTS

In Greece, researchers **counted the dimples on the cheeks** of 28,282 kids. This is what they found out:

- approximately 13% of Greek children have dimples.

- girls and boys have about the same amount of dimples.

- kids with dimples in their left cheek are as common as kids with dimples in their right.

- only 3.5% of kids have dimples in both cheeks.

- Greek adults have about three times more dimples than children do.

Scientists in Taiwan say they have bred **pigs that glow in the dark**! The pigs were created in experiments that took genetic material from jellyfish (which glow with a greenish light) and inserted it into normal pig embryos. The result: three green pigs that supply their own night lights. (That should keep the Big Bad Wolf at bay until morning!)

ON THE LOOSE

What is the vilest, most horrible smell in the world?
Researchers have been hard at work, and here's what they've sniffed out:

- butyl seleno-mercaptan (C4H9SeH): The stuff that makes skunks' spray stinkaroo. Hoo-eee! While it is not toxic, it smells bad enough that you might think it were.

- "U.S. Government Standard Bathroom Malodor": Swirl eight really yucky molecules together. The result could be this fragrant chemical, developed by American chemists to test the effectiveness of air fresheners and deodorizers.

- "Who-Me?": Yup, that's the real name of this sulfur-based chemical that smells like dead animals. It was developed during World War II. French resistance fighters would use it to humiliate German soldiers by making them stink. It didn't really work. The French found it was hard to apply to the intended target without getting sprayed too.

Can people **smell each other's fear**?
Scientists at the University of Vienna, in Austria, performed a frightful experiment to find out. A group of women were asked to watch both scary and boring movies. While they watched the movies, they wore absorbent pads in their armpits to collect their sweat. Later, the sweat-soaked pads were given to another group to sniff. The sniffers were able to identify the pads worn during the scary movie more often than chance alone would predict. The researchers concluded that a specific chemical appears in sweat only when people are frightened.

ONE AND ONLY YOU

Do you have hair like your mother? Or eyes like your father? If you do, you can thank your genes. Genes are sets of chemical instructions for how you are made, a kind of "recipe" for building a body. Genes are passed from one generation to another in parts of your cells called chromosomes. Your genes are yours and yours alone. Except for identical twins, no two people—not even those with the same parents—will have exactly the same combination.

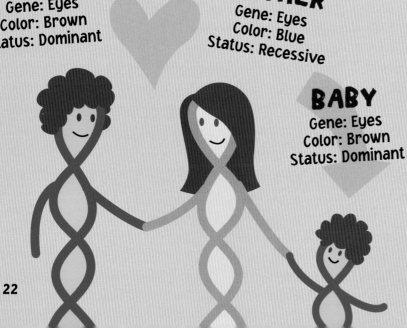

FATHER
Gene: Eyes
Color: Brown
Status: Dominant

MOTHER
Gene: Eyes
Color: Blue
Status: Recessive

BABY
Gene: Eyes
Color: Brown
Status: Dominant

Dominant or Recessive?

You have two copies of every gene: one from each parent. Some genes, such as the one for curly hair, come in two forms—dominant or recessive. The characteristics of a recessive gene can come out only when each parent passes along a recessive gene, so that both genes in the pair are recessive. A dominant gene's traits will come through if one or both in the pair are dominant. If you have one or two copies of the dominant gene version for curly, you will have curly hair. With two recessive genes, it will be straight.

MYSTERY GENE HUNT

Genes control a lot of how your body works. They determine how long your bones may grow and the shape of your fingernails. They even affect whether you are shy or crave excitement. Which genes do you have? Some, like the ones that determine hair or eye color, are easy to discover. Other genes, however, are harder to spot. Take a dip in the gene pool with some simple experiments that will help you to uncover some of your own mystery genes.

YOU'LL NEED

a mirror (for some of the tests)

Tongue Test:
Can you curl your tongue into a U shape? 70% of us can. What about a clover leaf? That tongue-twisting ability is much less common.

Hitchhiker's Thumb Test:
Can you bend your thumb backwards at an angle of more than 45 degrees? Only 25% of the population can!

Toe Test:
Which is longer, your "thumb" (big) toe or your second toe? If your second toe is longer, you are in the minority.

Ear Lobe Test:
Are yours detached, or do your earlobes connect right to the side of your head? More than 70% of the population has free-hanging earlobes.

Twiddler Test:
Interleave your fingers and fold your hands in your lap. Which hand's thumb and index finger are on top? For 75% of people, it's the left thumb and index finger.

Dracula Test:
Does your hairline come to a point on your forehead? This is usually called a "widow's peak." 75% of the population has one!

Hyper Humans

Test yourself: can you easily (don't strain!) bend in any of the ways shown here? If so, you are double-jointed! The term refers to joints that have "double" the normal range of motion. The scientific term is "hypermobility." If you are double-jointed, there are probably other people in your family who are too. The tendency toward hypermobility is a genetic trait passed directly from parent to child. Hypermobility can be great if you are a dancer or gymnast. Your loosey-goosey joints make you extra-flexible so you can do bouncier jumps and bendier bends. But hypermobile joints are also more vulnerable to injury and arthritis. Don't overextend your joints often if you want to keep them healthy. Follow up by finding out who else in your family has the same trait and draw up a genetic family tree.

I am SO the boss of you.

Eeep!

THE DOMINANT EYE TEST

1 Curl your thumb and index finger to form a circle.

2 Hold the circle in front of your face and look through it at a distant point. Whatever the object is, you should see it clearly inside your finger circle, with both your eyes.

3 Without moving the circle, close one eye, and then the other.

4 Does the object "jump" back and forth out of the circle? Which eye is the one that still sees the object through the circle? This is your dominant eye.

What's Going On?

Most people who are right-handed have a dominant right eye. Lefties tend to have a dominant left eye. Both handedness and eye-ness are evidence of which half of your brain is dominant (the opposite side from your dominant eye or hand). But not everybody has a dominant brain hemisphere. If you are right-handed and left-eyed, or vice versa, your brain's halves are sharing the work.

Left, Right, or Middle?

The left and right sides of your brain process information differently. The left side likes to think in straight lines, by looking at small parts first to build a whole picture. The right brain, however, sees the big picture first, not the details. It's good at reading faces and emotions; it likes to put ideas together in new ways, and come up with stories. "Left-brainers" tend to be logical and organized. "Right-brainers" tend to be creative and intuitive. "Middle-brainers" get the best of both worlds.

Does It Smell Left-Handed?

Some chemicals come in two different forms, called "mirror molecules." Like your two hands, they are the same, except for the direction they face. Mirror molecules can have different properties depending on whether they are "left-handed" or "right-handed." Strangely enough, how the molecules smell is one of those properties!

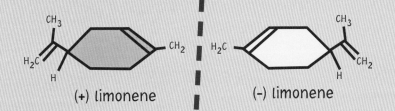

(+) limonene   (-) limonene

To see for yourself, sniff some grated lemon rinds, and then some grated orange rinds. Do they smell different? Both rinds contain a molecule called limonene, a mirror molecule. The chemical is the same, but it is left-handed in the orange rind, and right-handed in the lemon rind!

The smell receptors in your nose come in different shapes. So do odor molecules. When odor molecules go up into your nose, they pass over the smell receptors. If one of the molecules is the same shape as one of the receptors, it will fit into it, like a key into a lock. When a scent receptor "captures" an odor molecule, it sends a message to the brain. Depending on which receptors are triggered, the brain puts the messages together and matches them to a particular scent: "Aha!" it thinks. "That combination means orange." Because the two different forms of limonene face different directions, they don't fit the same smell receptors. So when you sniff a lemon and an orange, the signals your brain receives from your nose are different.

Cats and dogs, like humans, can be either lefties or righties. All polar bears are lefties.

Try It!

Do you have a dominant foot? Without thinking too much about it, walk up or down some stairs. Which foot did you lead off with? Is it the same side as your dominant hand or eye?

SMELLEBRATE YOUR INDIVIDUALITY

It would probably seem pretty strange if humans sniffed each other like dogs do when we met. But our sense of smell is actually a very important part of who we are and how we sense the world around us.

EAU DE YOU

Everyone has their own distinctive smell. Need proof? Try this simple sniff test for yourself.

YOU'LL NEED

1 plastic bag for each member of your family, including yourself

~

blindfold (optional)

~

friend(s) or family member(s)

~

black marker

~

pad and pencil

1 Using the black marker, label each bag: 1, 2, 3, etc.

2 Draw a simple table on your pad listing each bag number with columns beside it to write a name.

3 Ask each family member for a t-shirt they have worn once. It shouldn't be too dirty.

4 Put one shirt into each bag.

5 Cover your eyes with the blindfold or just close your eyes.

6 Have your friend or family member hold bag 1 close to your nose. Sniff. Guess which family member the clothing in the bag belongs to.

7 Write your guess (or have your friend write it for you) on your chart.

8 Repeat until you have sniffed all of the bags.

9 Check your answers. Were your guesses correct?

What's Going On?

Your personal scent is something you are born with. New moms can actually identify their infants simply by sniffing the tops of their heads! Blood chemistry, hormone levels, even the structure of your immune system, all work together to create your basic aroma.

When B.O. Is Good

Ever wonder why some people are more irresistible than others to mosquitoes? The answer is in their body odor (B.O.). We all emit smelly chemicals in our sweat. Those who get bitten less produce a particularly stinky chemical that masks the more attractive (to mosquitoes) odors. To find out which chemical it is, scientists in Scotland had different volunteers stick their arm in one end of a Y-shaped chamber. The mosquitoes could choose which arm smelled better, and fly down that branch of the Y. The scientists collected and analyzed the sweat of the people who got bitten least. The best B.O., they discovered, is as potent a mosquito repellant as synthetic products containing the toxic chemical DEET!

A Scent to Remember

Do certain smells trigger vivid memories for you? Smell is a special sense because, rather than being connected to the thinking part of your brain as your other senses are, smell is directly linked into your brain's emotion center. So catching a whiff of a particular odor can bring you right back to another time and place in your mind.

Who's Nosier?

On average, girls have a keener sense of smell than boys do.

P-U!

SMACK!

SEEING IS BELIEVING

Seeing is believing. Or is it?
Try these eye-luminating experiments to
find out more about your sense of vision.

THE GOOD PUPIL EXPERIMENT

Your eyes are top of the class when it comes to controlling light.

YOU'LL NEED

flashlight
~
mirror

1 Take a flashlight and a mirror into a darkened room.

2 Allow your eyes to adjust to the light.

3 Now look closely at your eyes in the mirror while you turn on the flashlight (do not point the flashlight at your eyes or the mirror). Do your pupils contract (get smaller)?

The opening and contracting of your pupils is controlled by the **pupillary reflex**. See page 16 for more on how reflexes work.

What's Going On?

Your pupils are the opening through which light passes into the eye. When you are in dark surroundings, the pupil opens wide to let more light in so you can see. When you turn on the flashlight, suddenly more light is coming into your eye—too much light! Ow! Your pupil shrinks, or contracts, to reduce the amount of light going into the eye.

I've Got My Eye On You...

If you know someone is watching you, you probably will behave better than if you are alone, right? But what if there's only a picture of someone watching you?

Researchers in Newcastle, England, wanted to find out if people paying for coffee on the honor system would be more or less likely to "cheat" when watchful eyes were present, even if the eyes were only in a picture. So they put up weekly price lists for coffee in their psychology department lounge. Sometimes the price list had a picture of flowers in it. Sometimes it had pictures of faces, with the eyes in each face looking directly at you. The prices on the list remained the same every week.

In the weeks when the price list showed a picture with the watching eyes, staff smartened up! They put 2.76 times more money in the collection box than when the price list had flowers on it.

Try It Yourself!
Cut out a picture from an old magazine of a face with eyes that seem to stare at you. Post it somewhere in your house. Do people behave differently in front of the picture? Do you?

Glow in the Dark Science

Did you know that you can identify different animals by what color their eyes glow at night? Can you match the eyes to the animals below? (Note that two of the animals have green eyes.) Answers on page 63.

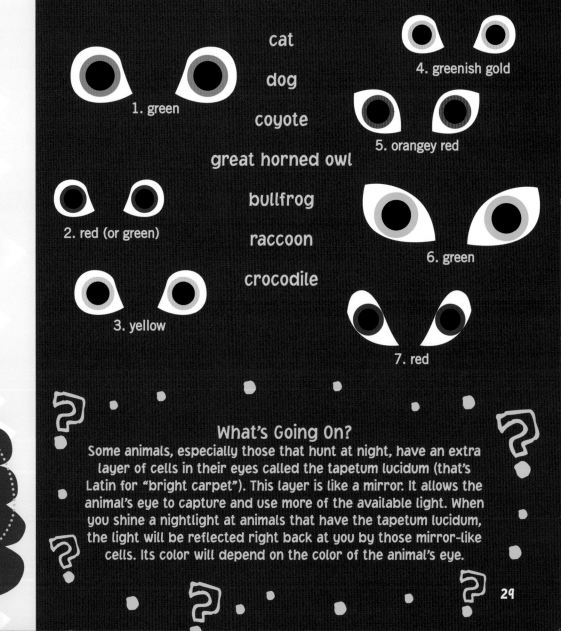

cat

dog

coyote

great horned owl

bullfrog

raccoon

crocodile

1. green

2. red (or green)

3. yellow

4. greenish gold

5. orangey red

6. green

7. red

What's Going On?
Some animals, especially those that hunt at night, have an extra layer of cells in their eyes called the tapetum lucidum (that's Latin for "bright carpet"). This layer is like a mirror. It allows the animal's eye to capture and use more of the available light. When you shine a nightlight at animals that have the tapetum lucidum, the light will be reflected right back at you by those mirror-like cells. Its color will depend on the color of the animal's eye.

MORE EYE-XCITING EYE-XPERIMENTS

THE MAGICALLY REAPPEARING GHOST

The ghosts want to get into the house at the right. Can you use nothing but the magic of your eyes to put the ghosties into the haunted mansion?

1. Stare at the ghosts on the left for 10 to 15 seconds.

2. Shift your eyes quickly to the haunted house. Do you see shadowy, light-colored ghosts inside the house?

What's Going On?

When you stare at a colored image, like these ghosts, the receptors in your retina for that color get "fatigued," and temporarily do not work properly. Then, when you look at a different colored background (the purple haunted house), the receptors that got tired can't "see" purple anymore. So you see an identical image in another color, usually pink or green. These lingering "after-images" last about 5 seconds.

Dazzled by the Light

Did you ever notice when you come inside on a bright day, it's suddenly hard to see, and everything appears to be either pink or green? There are two factors at work when this happens. First of all, your pupils need to dilate, or open up, to adjust to the new, darker conditions. (See the quickie experiment on page 28.) You are also seeing after-images from whatever you were looking at outside. Very bright light and lots of contrast —the conditions on a bright, sunny day—make the strongest after-images.

Under-See Creatures?

Your eyeballs measure about 2.5 cm (1 in.) in diameter. The largest eyes in the world belong to the **giant squid**. The squid's eyes each measure about 25 cm (10 in.) across. That's about the size of a volleyball!

EYE SEE NOW

SPINNING WHEEL ILLUSION

If you don't look directly at it (look just above or below or to the side), does it look like the wheel in the image at left is spinning backwards?

What's Going On?

This optical illusion is caused by tiny little motions of your eyes. Focus hard on one part of the picture to stop your eye movement. The wheel will stop moving too.

Spinning Backwards?

Did you ever look at a bicycle wheel, a hubcap on a car tire, or even a fan, and get the impression that it was spinning in the opposite direction from which it was really turning? This is a very common optical illusion.

We think we perceive a constant stream of information through our eyes. In fact, your brain can only process information in tiny bits. It's as if your brain takes many snapshots, then mentally fuses them together into one smooth film.

Now imagine you are watching an object such as a spoked bicycle wheel spin. Your brain takes "snapshots" of the wheel. There are small gaps between each shot, just like when you snap several photographs in a row.

RUNNING LATE? STOP THAT CLOCK!

Need proof that there are gaps in your inner film (see "Spinning Backwards?" below)? Try this easy experiment.

1 Look at a clock face.

2 Watch the second hand move for a few seconds.

3 Look away for a second, then back to the clock.

4 Does the second hand seem to "hang" for a second before resuming its motion? If so, you've just glimpsed the gap! The second hand will resume its "normal" speed when your brain starts supplying the information to hide the gap again.

Meanwhile, the wheel keeps turning. It's not in the same position the next time your brain snaps its mental picture. Your brain tries to make sense of the new, slightly different image by locking onto a spoke that is closest to a spoke it remembers from the previous snapshot. If the wheel is turning fast enough, that spoke might be the one behind the original spoke. Your eye jumps to it, **moving in the opposite direction** to which the wheel is turning.

Repeat this sequence several times, and your eye "sees" the wheel spinning backwards!

SCIENTISTS

THE ANIMAL CRACKERS FILES

A Canadian experiment suggested that **dogs can sniff out humans who have bladder cancer**! The dogs were able to identify the people with the disease by the smell of their urine.

SNIFF

Scientists at Stockholm University in Sweden came up with an experiment that determined **"Chickens Prefer Beautiful Humans."** This was the actual title of the research report published in the prestigious science journal *Nature*.

ON THE LOOSE

Pop star Peter Gabriel spent time at a scientific research center in Georgia studying bonobo apes. The aim of his experiment was to find out if he could **teach the apes how to play the keyboards**! If the results are good, Gabriel plans to record and release the ape "music" on his own record label.

Mmmmmm...

Shop 'n' Sniff
Order Now!
Cookies by the dozen

Engineers at the Tokyo Institute of Technology are building **a machine that can record and play back fragrances**. Simply point the device at a freshly baked cookie, for example, and it will sniff out its unique chemical signature, using microchips. Then, a set of 96 non-toxic chemicals can be combined in a unique digital "recipe" to recreate and replay the scent.

SLEEPY TIME SCIENCE

Think about yawning for the next ten seconds. Picture a big, wide, mouth-stretching yawn. While you are picturing that yawn, keep in mind that everybody yawns: babies and grownups, birds, and mammals. It's a great big yawn of a world. Did you feel like yawning while you read the words above? Congratulations—you've just helped prove that yawning is contagious.

This One's a Real Yawner

The year 1942 must have been a very dull year. That's when the first scientific experiment to show that yawning is contagious took place. Scientist Joseph Moore trained researchers to imitate realistic looking yawns. He then planted them in public places, such as libraries and school assemblies. He discovered that seeing someone yawn—or even just hearing one—was enough to make most people break out in yawns of their own.

Try This:
Next time you're on a bus or at the library, try yawning and seeing if it makes others around you start yawning too.

IN THE ANIMAL WORLD

Some animals, such as chimpanzees and orangutans, may also be susceptible to contagious yawning. They, like humans, are capable of understanding what other individuals might be thinking or feeling.

YOU'LL NEED

someone to bring you to the zoo

a notebook and pencil or pen

1 Settle yourself next to the chimpanzee or orangutan enclosure at your local zoo.

2 Make some loud, exaggerated yawns. Do the animals yawn back?

3 Keep track of the number of times you yawn, and the number of times your subject yawns.

4 Record your findings in a science notebook.

Catch These Sleepy Facts...

Some scientists say the infectious nature of yawning may have **evolved** as a kind of signal that alerted the group when it was time to go to sleep.

Scientists have shown that people who are most susceptible to contagious yawns are better able to see things from another's **point of view** than those who don't catch yawns.

New research says yawning may act as a **brain-cooling** mechanism! Like computers, our brains operate more efficiently when cool. A big yawn brings more blood flow and cooler air to your brain.

People yawn more when they are **bored or tired**.

Most yawns last about **6 seconds**.

You can start catching yawns when you are between one and **two years old**.

Again with the same old story...!

Humans start yawning at **11 weeks** after conception. That's about 6 months before the baby is even born!

FOOD FOR THOUGHT

Who says you shouldn't play with your food? Of course you should—in the name of science! If you are hungry for more science fun, then chew over some of the nutty experiments on the next few pages.

Smart Dessert?

A bowl of wiggly gelatin has brain waves identical to those of adult men and women. Really! Neurologist Adrian Upton, at McMaster University in Canada, attached electrodes to a bowl of lime Jell-o™. He recorded wave activity very similar to that of the human brain when attached to an EEG (electroencephalogram) machine. Upton said that although the portion of Jell-o™ he used was about the size of a human brain, it was not doing any thinking. The "brain" waves from the fruity gel were probably caused by the vibrations of various machines that were being operated nearby.

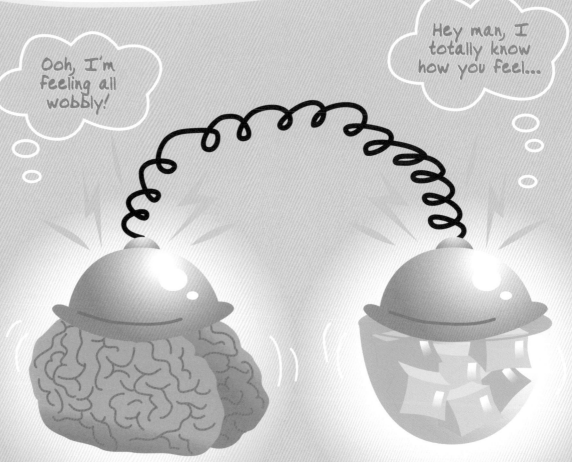

Ooh, I'm feeling all wobbly!

Hey man, I totally know how you feel...

FRUIT SINK OR SWIM

YOU'LL NEED

several varieties of fresh and canned fruit such as seedless grapes, chopped apple, sliced banana, strawberries, pears, apricots, and cherries

1 package gelatin mix

~

mixing bowl

~

measuring cup

~

hot water

~

mixing spoon

Why should the brainiacs at universities get to have all the gelatinous fun? Do your own experiment to find out which fruits will sink, and which will float. The best part: you can gobble it up when you're done!

1 Make gelatin according to the package directions.

2 Cool the prepared gelatin in the refrigerator for at least half an hour, or until it is partially set.

3 Sprinkle your fruit selections on top of the gelatin.

4 Return the bowl to the refrigerator.

5 When the gelatin has completely cooled, check out the fruit. Which has floated and which has sunk?

What's Going On?

Fruits that are denser—or have more mass—than a blob of gelatin the same size will sink. Fruits that are less dense—or have less mass—than a blob of gelatin the same size, will float. Denser fruits, like grapes and fruits that have been canned in heavy syrup, are full of water or juice. Less dense fruits, like fresh apples, bananas, citrus fruits, sliced peaches, pears, and strawberries, and fruit packed in light syrup contain more air.

Do **fruits and veggies have personalities**? They do according to research carried out at the University of California in 1988. From their experiments, researchers concluded that lemons are seen as unlikable, onions are not the smartest vegetable in the crisper, and mushrooms are trying to get ahead.

CHEW ON THIS

YUMMY TEST

Tickle your tastebuds with this flavorful experiment.

YOU'LL NEED

1 onion, chopped into small cubes

~

1 radish, chopped into small cubes

~

1 apple, whole

~

a friend

1 Close your eyes.

2 Hold your nose. This will take away most of your sense of smell, so you are relying on taste alone.

3 Have your friend give you a piece of either the onion or radish to taste. (Don't let your friend tell you which one!)

4 Try and guess which vegetable you are tasting.

Your sense of hearing, like your sense of taste, can be affected by context. Think about a time when you saw a ventriloquist using a dummy. Did it really sound like the voice was coming from the dummy? The next time you see a ventriloquist perform, close your eyes. If you don't see the dummy's mouth moving, the illusion will disappear!

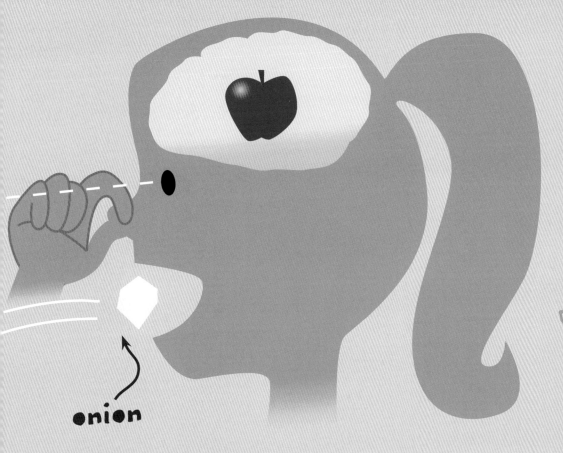

onion

What's Going On?

Your brain takes in information all around you: what you hear, smell, and see. It makes sense of the world by trying to put all that information into one idea that makes sense. This is called "context." If you see an apple, your brain automatically matches what it sees to what it knows about apples. When you mix up the context, your brain has trouble processing the information. It sees and smells the apple...so why wouldn't it taste apple? It will, even if you are actually eating the onion!

5 Now, open your eyes and place the apple in front of you.

6 Repeat the experiment three more times: first, while looking at the apple, then holding the apple, then smelling the apple.

7 Can you tell what vegetable you are tasting? Does it taste like apples? Which version of the experiment gives you the strongest taste of apple?

COOL SCIENCE!

Finding out the answers to science mysteries can be totally sweet.
Check out this experiment to savor the flavor.

KICK THE CAN ICE CREAM

Want to experiment with ice cream on your own? You'll get a "kick" out of
this easy—and delicious!—recipe!

YOU'LL NEED

one 454 g (1 lb)
empty coffee can with lid

~

one 1.4 kg (3 lb)
empty coffee can with lid

~

duct tape

~

scissors

~

250 mL (1 cup)
whole milk

~

250 mL (1 cup)
half & half cream

125 mL (1/2 cup)
sugar

~

5 mL (1 tsp)
vanilla extract

~

250 mL (1 cup)
rock salt

~

1 L (4 cups)
crushed ice

~

mixing spoon

~

measuring cup

1 Mix together the milk, cream, sugar, and vanilla extract in the smaller coffee can.

2 Put the lid on the can and, using the duct tape, seal it really, really, really well. Be sure to seal both the top and bottom of the can so the liquid doesn't leak out.

3 Put the taped can into the larger coffee can.

4 Fill the space between the inside of the large can and the smaller can with the crushed ice all the way to the top. Add the rock salt to the ice.

Only **30%** of the general population suffers from ice cream headaches, while **90%** of migraine sufferers do.

The average brain freeze headache lasts about 5 to 15 **seconds**. Get rid of one faster by warming the roof of your mouth with your tongue.

Icy C-o-o-l Science

What's the deal with brain freeze—that headache you get when you eat ice cream too fast? Dr. Robert Smith, at the University of Cincinnati's Headache Center, decided to find out. He tried this experiment: he placed crushed ice in his mouth, way back against the palate. And, yup—he got brain freeze. Why? Smith thinks that when you eat or drink super-cold foods, the nerve center at the back of your mouth suddenly thinks your brain is getting too cold. So it sends a message to release more blood to the area around the brain to warm it. The extra blood causes a headache similar to a migraine.

What's Going On?

Cream, like water, freezes at 0°C (32°F). So at that temperature liquid cream turns into ice cream. Putting ice around the cream chills it. At the same time, though, the ice gets warmer, and starts to melt. Once the ice melts, it's no longer cold enough to freeze the cream. But when you add salt to the ice, the situation changes. Because salt water freezes at a much colder temperature than fresh water (at -6.7°C/20°F) it's going to take a lot more heat energy to melt that salty ice! The cream gets colder, colder, colder...down below 0°C (32°F). Hooray—dessert!

5 Tape the lid of the large coffee can in place tightly with the duct tape. Again, seal everything up well to prevent leaks.

6 Get some pals together and play a game of kick the can outside on a grassy area. If the weather isn't great, you can take turns shaking the can while singing and dancing to your favorite tunes.

7 Keep kicking or rolling until the ice cream is set. It will take 15 minutes to half an hour.

8 Use scissors to cut the tape from the coffee cans.

9 Lift the smaller can out, being careful not to get any of the salty ice water from between the two cans in your ice cream!

10 If the ice cream is still a bit mushy in the center, you can put it in the freezer, just until it firms up.

11 Enjoy! If you have any leftovers (not likely), transfer to a plastic container to store in the freezer.

Serves up to 4 ice cream lovers.

SCIENTISTS

KOOKY KITCHEN SCIENCE

These cookies are pretty crumby.

Staff at the McVitie's laboratory in England designed the perfect machine for testing their world famous cookies. They called it the **Crumb Test Dummy**. The dummy was used to find out which baking techniques produced cookies that made the most crumbs. The robot has plastic teeth and can chomp cookies all day without getting a sugar high or putting on one extra pound, or even needing to stop for breath.

Uh, oh. **You dropped your toast.** Which way is it going to land— butter side up, or butter side down? After 10,000 tumbling toast trials, a physicist at Aston University in England discovered that gravity and friction cause toast to fall butter side down 62 per cent of the time. So it's not just your own bad luck!

cookie-bot V.3

ON THE LOOSE

A science teacher hooked up a pickle to a pair of electrodes. To her surprise, not only did the pickle start to sizzle, but it also gave off an unearthly glow. The question was why. It took several years and many researchers to finally solve the mystery of the **glowing pickle**! It turns out it's actually the pickle vapor that shines. The vapor is the heated brine, or salty water, the pickle soaks in. When energy is added to the pickle, in the form of electricity, it excites the sodium ions (salt) in the pickle vapor. The electrons in the vapor begin to jump around. They move to a higher orbit in the sodium atoms. When the pickle starts to cool off, the atoms go back down to where they belong. They let go of the excess energy, by releasing packets of photons. You see the photons in the form of yellow light. But don't look for pickle lightbulbs any time soon. Scientists also discovered that hot pickles smell really bad!

Scientists at Cornell University placed clear **jars of chocolates** on some people's desks. They placed opaque jars of chocolates on other people's desks. Guess which people ate more candy? Yup. Those who could see the sweets ate twice as much as those who couldn't!

SILLY STATES OF MATTER

Matter comes in three forms, or states: solid, liquid, and gas.
Some would say gas is the funniest of the three. Let's see if you agree.
Like other scientists before you, you can have a blast researching gas.

Beans, Beans, Good for Your Heart...

Scientists in Australia conducted an experiment to discover if beans really do make people pass more wind. Subjects counted how many times they—ahem—farted for two days. On day one, they ate a normal breakfast. On day two, they ate baked beans for breakfast. Here are the results of the experiment:

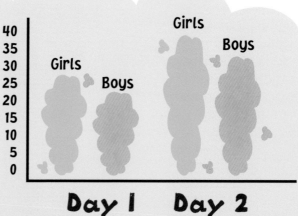

Average Number of Farts

40
35
30
25
20
15
10
5
0

Girls Boys   Girls Boys

Day 1   Day 2

- beans caused 51% of the test subjects to fart

- the next most popular gas inducer: soda pop (43% said the bubbles made them bubble)!

IT'S NOT ME, IT'S THE BEANS

1 Create the following chart on a piece of paper and make 10 copies (one for each participant):

2 Hand a chart to each of your friends who will be taking part in the experiment. You can tell them that they do not have to write their name on their chart (to avoid embarrassment), but they MUST write whether the chart belongs to a boy or a girl.

3 Ask your volunteers to eat a normal breakfast on day one of the experiment. Using the chart, have all the volunteers keep track of every time they pass wind during that entire day.

4 On the second day of your experiment, have the same volunteers eat baked beans for breakfast. Have them track the number of times they pass wind during this second day too.

5 Collect the completed records from each volunteer. Make sure each sheet says whether the volunteer who collected the data was a boy or girl.

6 Tally the total number of farts recorded for day one on each chart.

7 Tally separately the total number of farts recorded for day two on each chart.

8 Make a chart with 4 columns, Day 1, broken down into girls and boys and then Day 2, girls and boys

9 Put the totals from each volunteer's chart in the appropriate column.

10 Add up the figures in each column.

11 Which column has a higher number for day one, the girls or boys? Which column has a higher total for day two, girls or boys? Which column has the highest total altogether? Do your findings agree with the Australian study?

Matter in Motion

Did you know that if you had an infinite amount of time, you could, in theory, **walk through a wall**? Here's how: all substances, including you, are made up of atoms. And 99.9999999999999% of an atom's volume is just empty space. Except at the very coldest temperatures (called Absolute Zero), the atoms in everything around us are always moving. Gases have the fastest moving atoms. Liquids have atoms that move less quickly than gases, but faster than solids. Solid objects, such as a wall and your body, are also full of moving atoms. They just move v-e-r-y s-l-o-w-l-y. Since the atoms are moving, it's possible to sneak something in between them. You just have to time it right. Sooner or later—much, much, much later—you'd be able to squeak all of your atoms through the wall's atoms, and right through to the other side!

PLANET PLANT

Don't be fooled by that mild-mannered fern sunning itself by the kitchen window. People aren't the only living things that pass wind. Yup, plants do too! Find out more about our green pals' peculiar little habits when you enter the mysterious world of "Planet Plant."

Jungle Burps

Trees "inhale" carbon dioxide, reducing global warming, right? Maybe. A recent finding by scientists in Germany, the Netherlands, and Ireland suggests that the world's rainforests might not be quite so atmosphere-friendly. In fact, the researchers estimate that, globally, plants burp out up to 30% of the world's methane emissions, contributing to global warming. That being said, the lead researcher on the project concludes that the plants still absorb more greenhouse gas than they produce.

Much worse in the burp department are cows. They account for nearly 20% of the methane gas in the atmosphere. That's a whopping 570 L (150 gallons) of gas a day for each cow on the planet! Don't worry, though, scientists are hard at work on an additive for cattle feed that will reduce cows' flatulence.

Think methane is a big problem? Here's a heads-up: a global study found that tiny flakes of "biological detritus" (a.k.a. dandruff) are a much more significant part of the atmosphere. Air samples collected over Germany, Siberia, the Amazon rainforest, Greenland, and remote oceans found that dandruff can make up about 25% of all atmospheric particles. In fact, there are so many flakes out there that they may even affect the weather.

Mighty Oaks or Major Hoax?

Do you think plants feel fear? A famous experiment conducted in 1966 concluded that they do. But was the experiment solid, or full of hot air?

Cleve Backster attached electrodes from a polygraph machine to a plant. The machine, called a "lie detector," is used to measure changes in the way human skin reacts to an electric current. These changes are thought to happen when a person feels stress when he or she tells a lie.

Once the plant was hooked up to the polygraph, Backster began a series of experiments, including dipping a leaf into warm coffee, to see if he could produce a reaction. The plant did nothing. Backster concluded that the plant was "bored." He then wondered what would happen if he set the plant's leaves on fire.

At that moment, the plant, he said, went "wild." The polygraph began producing readings similar to those produced by frightened people. Further experiments, Backster claimed, showed that plants could sense dying animals, and would react with terror to a person who has previously killed plants out of the "view" of the plant!

Unfortunately, Backster neglected to use proper scientific controls while conducting his experiment. Although his conclusions have been widely publicized, his experiments have never been reproduced under scientific conditions. How would you design an experiment to test this idea?

Pardon ME!

PFFFFT!!

Beans Fight Back!

Biologists at the University of Turin and the Max Planck Institute in Germany have found evidence that lima bean plants don't just stand there when an enemy attacks. When they sense the presence of leaf-chomping grubs, the bean plants react by giving off an odor similar to lavender. The smell not only alerts other plants in the area, but it also attracts wasps that feed on the unlucky grubs.

ANIMAL PLANET

DOLLY 1

It's not only plants that inhabit our planet. Our world is home to awesome animals. Did you know that some of the most fascinating animals of all are actually scientists? Meet the beasts who put the roar into lab-roar-atory.

The Koko Experiments

Project Koko is the longest-running experiment to study communication between two different species. In 1972 researcher Penny Patterson began working with a one-year-old female lowland gorilla named Koko. Penny taught her to use sign language to communicate and to respond to spoken English. Koko now has a working vocabulary of over 1,000 signs and understands about 2,000 words of spoken English. Koko has even combined words she knows to describe objects for which she didn't know the name. For example, she combined the signs for "eye" and "hat" to describe a mask, and "white" and "tiger" to describe a zebra.

Duck, Duck, Mom?

Imagine you are a duckling just emerging from your shell. How do you know who your mother is? It's simple—it's that really big object waddling in front of you. Most of the time, if you are a normal duck, that big object really is your mother. But what if it is a chicken, or a bearded man, or even a rubber ball?

Scientist Konrad Lorenz found out that the ducklings can't tell the difference! They, like many other animals, become "imprinted" on the first large moving object they see. Once imprinted, they will always treat that object like their mother. The hatchlings in Lorenz's experiment "imprinted" on him, and followed him around as if he were a parent bird.

Ian Had a Little Lamb...or Two

The most famous experiment involving an animal is undoubtedly the one conducted by Ian Wilmut, a Scottish scientist, in 1997. Wilmut made headlines when he announced he had cloned a sheep. Clones are created from the cells of an animal, put into a laboratory dish, and grown into a complete new animal. The cloned sheep, Dolly, became a "wool-wide" celebrity, but she died prematurely at the age of seven.

DOLLY 2

The first animals sent into space for scientific research were fruit flies, for an experiment to explore the effects of radiation. The **fruit flies**, alas, did not survive. It was a long thirteen years before any living beings that were sent into space actually made it back to Earth alive. The winners in the back-to-Earth lottery were Able, a rhesus monkey, and Baker, a squirrel monkey. They made the successful round-trip on *Jupiter AM-18*, traveling at speeds of more than 16,000 km (9,940 miles) an hour.

Harnessing Hamster Power!

As part of a science project, a 16-year-old boy in England invented a hamster-powered charger for a cell phone. He said his sister's hamster, Elvis, kept her awake for hours running in his exercise wheel. Thinking all that energy was going to waste, the boy rigged the wheel up to a system of gears and a turbine. For every two minutes that Elvis the Hamster spends in his exercise wheel, he generates thirty minutes of telephone talk time.

STICKY, SLIMY, STRONG...

Sometimes you've just got to roll up your sleeves and get gooey for science. You can experiment with some of these really goofy materials at home.

GOO

This goo is crazy! Is it solid? Is it liquid? Is it both?

YOU'LL NEED

250 mL (1 cup) water

~

500 mL (2 cups) cornstarch

~

food coloring (optional)

~

mixing bowl

~

measuring cup

1 If using food coloring, add a drop or two to the water.

2 Put the cornstarch in the mixing bowl. Gently pour the water over it.

3 Using your fingers, mix the water and cornstarch together.

4 Now you get to play with it! Keeping the goo in the bowl, push it around, stir it, smack it, drag your finger through it.

Note: This mixture can clog drains. Throw any leftover goo into a garbage bag.

What's Going On?

This mysterious mixture is sometimes a solid (if you slap it), but sometimes a liquid (if you stir it gently). In technical terms, it's a "non-Newtonian Fluid." All fluids have a property called viscosity, which describes how easily they flow. Honey and ketchup have high viscosity—they don't flow easily. Water has low viscosity—it flows well. According to Isaac Newton, a fluid's viscosity changes according to temperature. Think how much easier it is to pour warm honey. But the goo you've made does not change its viscosity when you change its temperature. It's non-Newtonian. It changes when force is applied, like when you smack it. Another non-Newtonian fluid you know is quicksand.

GOOP

Yup, another non-Newtonian fluid. But it's just a lot more fun to call it "Goop."

YOU'LL NEED

30 mL (2 tablespoons) white glue, such as Elmers

~

10 mL (2 teaspoons) boric acid (available in the laundry section of the supermarket, where it is called Borax, or in the natural remedies section of the drug store)

~

30 mL (2 tablespoons) water

~

1 drop your choice of color food coloring (optional)

~

mixing bowl

~

measuring spoons

~

mixing spoon

1 Mix all ingredients except the boric acid together and stir well.

2 Add the boric acid.

3 Stir until all ingredients are combined and the goop becomes slimy and disgusting.

4 When you make additional batches, experiment with the ratio of borax to glue. By changing the amounts of each, you can make your goop either bouncy and rubbery, or liquidy and revoltingly slippery. Both versions are fun.

5 Keep a record of the quantities you use when making each batch so you can duplicate your favorite slime in the future.

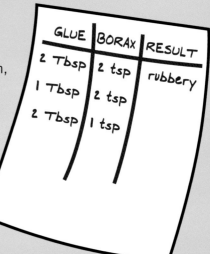

GLUE	BORAX	RESULT
2 Tbsp	2 tsp	rubbery
1 Tbsp	2 tsp	
2 Tbsp	1 tsp	

What's Going On?

White craft glue is a type of polymer, a material made up of a long chain of molecules. The chains are like strands of spaghetti. When borax is added to the glue, the borax molecules get tangled in the strands of glue. The glue can't flow freely any more. It becomes another non-Newtonian fluid, like Goo and quicksand. Goop needs heat in order to bond. When you stir the mixture, the heat energy from your hands is transferred to the mixture, making the glue and borax regroup into Goop.

Try This:

Test the effect of your hot little hands by letting the slime sit for a bit in the cup. Does it go all runny after a while? Get back that slimy feeling by stirring it again. The more you supply heat (by stirring), the more goopy it will get.

...AND STRETCHY

boing!

boing!

boing!

GREAT GALLOPING GLOP

Gluey glop is fun for everyone, even scientists. Here's a third version of a—you guessed it!—non-Newtonian fluid. Which one is your favorite?

YOU'LL NEED

2.5 mL (1/2 teaspoon) epsom salts (available in the bath section of the drug store)

~

2.5 mL (1/2 teaspoon) water

~

15 mL (1 tablespoon) white glue, such as Elmers

~

2 small mixing bowls or cups

~

measuring spoons

~

mixing spoon

1 Combine the epsom salts and water in the mixing bowl.

2 Stir until the epsom salts are dissolved.

3 Put the white glue in the second mixing bowl.

4 Add the epsom salt/water mixture to the glue.

5 Stir. A sticky, putty-like substance will come together!

SPLAT!

Stretchy Spider Stuff

Uri Gat, a biologist at the Hebrew University in Jerusalem, may just be the real Spiderman. He's produced the first artificial spiderweb fibers in a lab by injecting silk-making genes into cultured caterpillar cells. Since spider silk is the strongest natural fiber known—six times stronger than steel and super-stretchy to boot—the artificial strands may one day be used for practical applications such as surgical thread, bulletproof vests, clothing, and optical fibers—the hair-thin glass strands that carry digital information over long distances and make telephone, cable, and internet connections possible.

Scientists have found a glue in the wild that is **three times stronger** than anything else out there. It's the stuff that lets slimy green algae stick to rocks in a stream. The single-cell bacteria, called *Caulobacter crescentus*, uses sugar molecules and proteins to make the glue. It's so strong that two cars, driving in opposite directions, couldn't pull it apart! There's only one problem with the super glue—it's so sticky the scientists studying it can't wash the glue off their instruments!

The next time someone decides to start a riot, they might want to think twice. Researchers in Texas are working on a new **crowd control method**—slime. Riot police would wear a backpack containing water and a powdered polymer. A nozzle with two separate jets would shoot the stuff at unruly crowds. When the mixture comes in contact with air, it combines to form a super-slippery goo that would cause the troublemakers to trip, slip, and flop. Because the goop is non-toxic, it would cause no long-term harm.

In 1943, James Wright was trying to develop a synthetic form of rubber for the American war effort. He mixed boric acid with silicone. The result? Well—it wasn't rubber. It was a **weird bouncy glop** that sure was fun! That's how Silly Putty™, one of the world's most popular toys, was born. It was such a smash hit, that in 1968, the astronauts on *Apollo 8* actually brought the silly stuff with them to the Moon! Two eggs containing Silly Putty™ were even displayed in a special exhibit at the Smithsonian Museum in Washington, D.C.

How did rubber get its name? When Europeans were first introduced to this unusual material, they discovered that if they **rubbed** the stuff over texts written in pencil, the rubber would **erase** the words!

SPACED-OUT SCIENCE

Twinkling stars…dashing comets…gorgeous galaxies….
Isn't just thinking about space inspiring? Let's be honest. Most scientists like
to study space because that's where all the wackiest science takes place.

SPACE DIMPLES

YOU'LL NEED

4 friends

~

a tennis ball

~

a can of soup

~

a bedsheet

**Did you know that outer space is full of dimples?
Try this dippy experiment to see a space dimple for
yourself, and to find out why space dimples are really,
really important to you.**

1 Have your friends hold
the sheet stretched
out in the air. Place
the soup can in the
center. Does the sheet
dip with the weight
of the can, forming a
kind of dimple?

2 Now, with the can still
in place, drop a tennis
ball onto the sheet. What
happens? Probably the
ball rolls down the slope
into the dimple in the
sheet. Guess what? You've
just demonstrated gravity!

Gravity in Action

Gravity is the force that pulls
objects with mass toward each
other. They move toward each other
because of the way objects deform
the fabric of space—like the soup
can on the bedsheet. The bigger
the object in the middle of the
sheet, the faster the ball will roll
toward the center—the stronger the
gravitational "pull." A pebble in the
middle of the sheet won't make the
tennis ball move very much. It has
a smaller gravitational pull than a
heavy brick would.

What's Going On?

Space is like the bedsheet. Objects in space all cause space to bend and dip around them. The bigger the objects, and the more mass they have, the bigger the dimple. In space, when a smaller object (say, a planet), passes near a larger object (say, a star), it can get caught in the dimple around the larger object. The smaller object "rolls" into the dimple, the way the ball rolled into the dip in the sheet, because of gravity. So why don't smaller objects crash into bigger ones once they roll into the dimple? Some do. But if objects are traveling fast enough, they won't roll all the way down the slope. Instead, they will keep rolling around the lip of the curve. Scientists call this trick "being in orbit."

Try This:

Create a model orbit with your ball and sheet. This time, instead of dropping the ball onto the sheet, roll it fast around the edge of the dimple. If the ball is whipping around fast enough, you should be able to see it go "into orbit"—roll around the edge of the dip—a few times before it slows down and dribbles toward the can. In space, there isn't much friction, so the object would take a really long time to slow down enough to fall out of orbit.

INTO THE BLACK HOLE

More Space Dimples

If you did the jell-o experiment on page 39, you already know that some objects are denser than others. Now imagine you take a large object, like a star, and you squish it. Keep squishing it until it is just a single infinitely tiny point. Can you imagine how dense it would be? Can you imagine how much gravity there might be? Scientists who study space have imagined that the gravitational force would be infinite. It would be so powerful, that not even light could escape from its grasp. It would be a **black hole**.

It's All Relative

The idea that large objects would bend space is an important part of Albert Einstein's Theory of Relativity. When he first came up with the idea, it was totally revolutionary. No one knew if it was true or baloney. It had to be tested. So how did scientists test Einstein's idea? In 1919, an astrophysicist named Arthur Eddington traveled to an island off the coast of Africa. Another group of astronomers went to Brazil. Both groups watched a solar eclipse. During the eclipse, the Sun passed in front of a group of stars called the Hyades cluster. The astronomers knew ahead of time the exact positions of all of those stars. As the light from the stars entered the Sun's gravitational force, they measured the stars' positions again. Their positions seemed to move! The "dimple" in space around the Sun actually bent the starlight! This experiment proved that Einstein's theory of relativity was correct. Einstein became an international celebrity, literally overnight!

Try This:

You can make an object denser by squishing it into a smaller and smaller space. Take a dry sponge and lay a few rubber bands on top of it. Toss the sponge into some water (make sure the rubber bands don't fall off). The sponge floats, at least until it starts soaking up some water. That's because it's less dense than the water. Now take another dry but soft sponge and squish it into a ball. Tie it up with the rubber bands so it stays squished. Toss it in the water. Does it still float? The squished sponge has the same mass as the regular sponge, but is denser so it should sink.

The edge of a black hole is called the event horizon. Anything that crosses it would get sucked into the black hole and could never get back out.

If you looked across the rim of a black hole as you were going into it, you would see the back of your own head on the other side! Why? The light going into the hole gets so bent by the gravitational force that it bounces all the way around the rim to where you can see it!

Black holes can form when a neutron star, a star that has collapsed so it is small and dense (imagine a star with the mass of our Sun smushed into the city limits of Chicago), collapses even further.

Black Hole Facts

Many astronomers think there may be a black hole at the center of every galaxy!

A black hole the size of the Sun would take 10^{66} (that's a ten with 66 zeros behind it) years to evaporate.

If you were sucked into a black hole, the part that went into the hole first, say, your feet, would get pulled by the gravitational field with more force than the body parts that went in last, say, your head. You'd be s-t-r-e-t-c-h-e-d o-u-t!!!! Yikes!

If you fall through a black hole in just the right way, you might not get torn into nano-shreds. You might pop out the other side—in another universe!

STAR GAZING

Release the Stars!

Did you know that inside every pencil, there's a trapped neutron star? To release it, draw a line! Pencil "lead" is actually a form of pure carbon called graphite. Graphite is made of interlinked and stacked sheets of carbon. If you separate the stacks into layers only one atom thick, you'd have a material called graphene. Graphene is a lot like the stuff that makes up collapsed, or neutron, stars. Just think: each pencil mark you make has star potential!

TIME TRAVELER

Ready to travel through time? There. You just did. You are now in what used to be the future, but is now the present. Oops! That future's gone again. The former future and present is now the past! Ok, ok. So maybe that's not the kind of time travel you were thinking of. If you're thinking of something more exotic, you can do that too. Here's how: get moving really fast. Really fast. The faster you move through space, the slower you move through time. So if you are traveling at high speed—close to the speed of light—you will actually age more slowly than you do when you stand still! (Scientists have tested this by putting super-accurate clocks on high speed airplanes.)

Space and time are **connected**. You can't have one without the other. The fancy name for this idea is the Spacetime Continuum.

Can you do serious science experiments without even getting out of bed? Sure! When someone asked **Albert Einstein** where his laboratory was, he pointed to his pen. This was Einstein's way of saying "I do experiments in my imagination." In fact, Einstein came up with his Special Theory of Relativity simply by picturing in his mind what would happen if he were riding on a beam of light. Today, many far-out scientific ideas are developed in just this way, by doing "thought experiments." Of course, these same ideas take a lot of work to prove, usually with page after page of mathematical equations. And you'll probably want to get out of bed—to collect your Nobel Prize in Physics, of course!

Exploring Wormholes

Imagine space is a sheet of foam. You already know that objects with mass can bend space, right? So now imagine a massive object is dropped onto your foam spacesheet. It bends the space so much it forms a U with the ball at the bottom. A space dimple, like the one on your bedsheet. The space inside the U is called hyperspace.

Now imagine a second, smaller mass on one side of the U, and a third mass on the opposite side. The two additional masses would also bend space, making two small dimples in the sides of the spacetime U. Eventually, the smaller dimples might join up, making a tunnel from one side of space to the other! Voila! A wormhole.

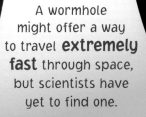

throat

mouth

A wormhole might offer a way to travel **extremely fast** through space, but scientists have yet to find one.

Where AM I?

Think about it: you've just traveled through a wormhole of your own—this book. As you read, you moved from the past to the future. You started with a discussion of you, and have ended up with a discussion of the frontiers of space. Along the way you experienced some of the strangest experiments science can offer. Has this book whetted your appetite for more wacky science? Then grab a hypothesis, gear up your theories, and get to work on your wonderfully weird experiments. Who knows where they'll take **you-u-u-u-u-u.....**

SCIENCE CONCEPTS

You probably thought this book was just loads of fun. But, of course, it was loaded with lots of great science too. Here is a list of scientific topics and experiments covered in *Science on the Loose*.

List of Experiments You Can Do

Answers

Glow in the Dark Science, page 29: cat=(6) green eyes; dog=(2) red or green eyes; coyote=(4) greenish gold eyes; great horned owl=(5) orangey-red eyes; bullfrog=(1) green eyes; raccoon=(3) yellow eyes; crocodile=(7) spooky red eyes

INDEX